MERLIN THE WIZARD

Retold by Ann Lawrence
Illustrated by Susan Hunter

Methuen Children's Books
in association with Belitha Press Ltd.

Note: Fragments of Merlin's story are found in many places. This story is based on the principal accounts: *The History of the Kings of Britain* by Geoffrey of Monmouth, *Le Morte d'Arthur* by Sir Thomas Malory, and the Old French tale *Le Roman de Merlin*.

AL

Art Director: Treld Bicknell
First published in Great Britain in 1986
by Methuen Children's Books Ltd,
11 New Fetter Lane, London EC4P 4EE
Conceived, designed and produced by Belitha Press Ltd.
31 Newington Green, London N16 9PU
ISBN 0 416 96130 4 (hardback)
ISBN 0 416 96140 1 (paperback)
Printed in Hong Kong by South China Printing Co.

AFTER THE ROMANS LEFT BRITAIN, Vortigern made himself King by treachery. The rightful King was deposed, and his young brothers, Aurelius Ambrosius and Uther, were smuggled away to Brittany for safety.
Vortigern was not allowed to enjoy his stolen crown in peace.

He was harassed by enemies, and lived in fear of the young princes.
He tried to make an alliance with the Saxons.
The Saxon leader, Hengist, proposed a conference.
The Britons went to it unarmed,
but all the Saxons carried hidden knives.
At an agreed word, Hengist seized Vortigern,
and his men attacked the British leaders.
Though a few escaped most were killed,
and Vortigern made his whole kingdom over to the Saxons
in exchange for his life.
Vortigern fled into Wales, where, on the advice of his magicians,
he began to build a great fortress to shelter him should all else fail.
But when his masons began to lay the foundations,
the earth swallowed each day's work in the night.

VORTIGERN CONSULTED HIS MAGICIANS AGAIN.
They told him that the foundations would hold firm,
if sprinkled with the blood of a fatherless boy.
Messengers were sent out to search for such a child.
They had almost given up, when they came
to a town in Demetia, in south Wales.
Some boys were playing by the town gate.
Suddenly a quarrel broke out between two of them,
one taunting the other, because no one knew who his father was.
The messengers began to take an interest.
They learned that the boy was called Merlin,
and that, though his father was unknown,
his mother was the daughter of the King of Demetia
and lived in a convent in that same town.
The messengers took Merlin and his mother to Vortigern without delay.
Knowing that the boy's mother was nobly born,
Vortigern received her courteously,
and began to question her about her son's father.
She told an astonishing tale.
"I do not know who or what he is," she said.
"But I believe he is no living man.
I only know that someone in the form of a handsome young man
often came to me in the private rooms of the convent.
He appeared and disappeared without warning.
Sometimes he would talk to me without becoming visible at all.
He made love with me like a man, and so I became pregnant."

VORTIGERN FOUND THIS DIFFICULT TO BELIEVE,
and so he consulted the most learned scholar at his court,
to find out if what the woman said could be possible.
This wise man listened to the story carefully then said:
"I understand that this may have happened any number of times.
There are certain spirits living between the earth and moon,
which are partly like men and partly like angels in their nature.
It seems they can take mortal shape,
and it is quite possible that one such may have fathered this boy."
All this time Merlin had been listening intently
to everything that was said.
Now he went up to the King and asked
why he and his mother had been brought there.
The boy's manner was so compellingly direct, that Vortigern told
the truth, before he had time to think of saying anything else.
Merlin reacted with scorn.
"Fetch your magicians, and I'll prove them liars!" he said.
"This isn't a matter of magic, but engineering!"
The startled King did as Merlin said.
"You have recommended sacrifice out of ignorance,
because you don't really know
what is undermining the foundations of this tower,"
Merlin said to the assembled sages.
"Well, do you know what's hidden down there?
There must be something
preventing it from holding firm."

The magicians could make no reply, so the boy continued:
"Lord King, order your men to dig
where you are trying to build your tower.
You will find a pool, which is making the ground unstable."
It was done and the pool was found. "Drain the pool," said Merlin.
"At the bottom you'll find two hollow stones,
in which two dragons are sleeping."
Now there was something strange about his voice.
The words seemed to come against his will.
As Vortigern and Merlin stood above the drained pool,
two dragons, one red, one white,
emerged from the stones and began to fight.
The struggle went first one way then the other,
but the white gained steadily all the time.

"What does it mean?" the King whispered. Merlin wept.
"The red dragon is the people of Britain," he said.
"The white is the Saxons, who will overrun them."
Then he fell into a trance and prophesied many things
in strange images, which no one understood.
When at last he sat silent,
everyone present was filled with astonishment and fear.
Vortigern, however, was impressed by the boy's intelligence
and his readiness to speak frankly before the King.
"Tell me my own fate now," he said.
"You need no oracle for that," said Merlin wearily.
"Two dangers threaten you,
and it is not easy to see which you will avoid.
The Saxons pursue you, and Aurelius and Uther are landing even now.

NEWS OF AURELIUS AMBROSIUS' RETURN CAME THE NEXT DAY,
but by then Merlin had slipped away
under the cover of the confusion created
by his own dramatic pronouncements.
The Britons made Aurelius King.
He and his brother first hunted down Vortigern
and burned him in his own citadel,
then after a long, bitter campaign in which Hengist was slain,
they drove the Saxons into the far north.
Aurelius then set himself to restore the realm.
He travelled through the country
re-establishing the law and rebuilding the towns.
When he came to the city now called Salisbury,
he was shown the burial place of the British leaders
killed at Hengist's treacherous conference.
He was deeply moved, and wished to erect some fitting memorial.
However, no one could think of anything noble enough.

EVENTUALLY THE ARCHBISHOP OF CAERLEON REMEMBERED MERLIN.
"There is one who might have the ingenuity
to devise your monument," he told the King.
"Send for Merlin, who prophesied before Vortigern."
Merlin proved elusive. He had taken to a wandering life,
but he was found at last in a place to which he often returned,
beside a forest spring.
Yet when the King's messengers brought him to court,
Aurelius seemed hardly to take him seriously, and
he asked the young man to prophesy, as if for mere entertainment.
His reaction to Merlin's suggestion for the monument was open mockery.

"Fetch the Giants' Dance from Ireland?" he cried.
"Even if it could be done, why should we want to?
Aren't there big enough stones in Britain?"
Merlin sharply rebuked the King's laughter,
and explained that these huge stones had deep religious
significance and unique medicinal properties.
So convincing was his seriousness,
that the Britons decided to send an expedition to Ireland,
under the King's brother Uther, to bring back the Giants' Dance.

O N LEARNING THE REASON FOR UTHER'S INVASION,
the Irish were as incredulous as Aurelius had been,
for they knew as little of the stones' virtues as he had.
Nevertheless, they resolved that not a chip of the Dance should
be taken from Ireland, and met the British in force.
Uther was victorious in the battle, putting the Irish to flight,
after which the Britons went on to Mount Killaraus,
where the great stone circle stood.
The Britons were overawed by the stupendous structure.
The task of removing it seemed impossible,
but Merlin devised means to dismantle it
and ship the stones back to Britain,
where he directed their re-erection
at the site of the heroes' grave.
This feat established Merlin firmly in the King's respect.
After that Aurelius kept him at court,
so as to have his remarkable skills always at his disposal.

ONE OF VORTIGERN'S SONS, PASCHENT,
still held out against Aurelius,
and he now turned for help to the Irish,
who were angry over the taking of the Giant's Dance.
Paschent landed in Wales with the Irish,
at a time when Aurelius was ill,
so Uther and Merlin went to meet them.
They were still seeking the enemy,
when a great star appeared in the sky
three nights in succession.
A single beam shone from it, ending in a fireball
shaped like a dragon,
from which another ray stretched out over the whole land.
Uther called for Merlin and asked him
the significance of the star.
"Aurelius Ambrosius is dead," said Merlin, weeping.
"The dragon signifies yourself –
you will be victorious and rule all Britain.
The other beam is your son,
who will be the greatest warrior ever known.
Go forward now, or we are lost."
Although he doubted Merlin's prophecies,
Uther advanced on the enemy.
The barbarians were defeated, and Paschent was killed.
As Uther returned to Winchester, he was met by messengers with
the news that Aurelius had been treacherously poisoned.
Aurelius was buried in the Giant's Dance,
and Uther became King , taking a dragon for his standard.
From then on he was known as Uther Pendragon,
which means "dragonhead".

THE WARS AGAINST THE SAXONS CONTINUED.
One of Uther's finest leaders was Gorlois, Duke of Cornwall,
whose wife Ygraine was the most beautiful woman in Britain.
At Eastertide Uther held court in London,
to celebrate a great victory,
and there he saw Ygraine for the first time.
He was filled with love for her,
so that he could think of nothing else,
and paid attention to no other person. Gorlois saw this.
Angry and fearful, he fled the court without taking leave.
Uther was furious over this insult.
He ordered the Duke to return, and
when Gorlois refused, he swore revenge.
Uther led his army into Cornwall.

GORLOIS WAS NOT STRONG ENOUGH TO MEET HIM,
so he left his wife in his strongest castle, Tintagel,
and retreated himself to a fortified camp nearby.
There the King besieged him.
But Uther's love for Ygraine grew beyond measure
and tormented him day and night. He went to Merlin for advice.
"There is a way you might gain access to this woman,
if you are prepared to risk it," he said.
"I can change your appearance,
so that you will look like Gorlois.
You would then be admitted to Tintagel without questions.
But if you are to have your desire, you must give me mine.
You and Ygraine will have a son.
When he is born, give him to me to rear."
Uther agreed to everything, and he spent that night with Ygraine.

However, during the night
Gorlois tried to break through the besieging army.
In the fighting he was killed.
When she heard of the time and manner
of her husband's death, Ygraine was troubled,
and wondered who had come to her in his likeness,
but she kept everything to herself.
Uther then made peace with the Duchess,
and soon they were married.
When her child was born,
Merlin reminded Uther of his bargain.
Uther was willing now to accept Merlin's word without question.
The boy was handed over to Merlin, who took him secretly
to an honourable knight, called Sir Ector, to be fostered.
This he did because he knew that Uther would die
while his son was still a child,
and so the boy must be hidden to keep him safe
until he was old enough to claim the kingdom.

WITHIN TWO YEARS UTHER FELL SICK.
All his enemies united to attack the country,
while he was too weak to lead his army.
At first they were successful. Then Merlin said:
"You shall have one more victory,
but only if you are present in person.
Go with your army, even if you have to be carried in a litter."
So King Uther was carried to his last battle in a litter,
and returned to London victorious.
Three days later he died.
At the last he spoke of his son, Arthur,
but since no one had ever heard of this son,
it seemed there was no one to inherit the kingdom.

THERE FOLLOWED YEARS OF UNREST AND CONFUSION.
Merlin disappeared about his own affairs and was rarely seen,
until late one autumn he appeared before
the Archbishop of Canterbury,
and advised him to summon all the lords to London by Christmas.
The Archbishop knew that Merlin said nothing without a purpose,
and so he did as he suggested.
The tale of the marvellous sword in the stone,
and how the young Arthur proved himself King by drawing it out,
has been told many times.
All through the early years of Arthur's reign,
when he was constantly at war with rebels or invaders,
Merlin stayed at the King's side, guiding him.
However, once Arthur's enemies were defeated and his rule established,
Merlin went to Northumberland, to his own master, Blaise,
who had first schooled him in the arts
for which he had become famous.
Merlin told him about all Arthur's battles,
and he began a chronicle of Arthur's reign.
From then on Merlin was seldom at court, yet always turned up
at times and in places where he was least expected.
In those days of his young manhood,
Arthur often rode out alone, much to the alarm of his lords.
On one such expedition he fought with King Pellinore,
who beat Arthur badly, and might have killed him,
had not Merlin been at hand to rescue the King.
He took Arthur to a hermitage, where he had his wounds tended,
and rested for several days.
When they came to leave, Arthur realized that he had lost his sword.

"No matter," said Merlin.
"There is one near here, which you shall have."
They rode until they came to a lake.
To his astonishment, Arthur saw a white-clad arm
holding a handsome sword above the water.
"There it is," said Merlin,
At that moment they saw a young woman
walking across the surface of the lake. "Who is that?" said Arthur.
"That is Niniane, the Lady of the Lake," said Merlin.
"She lives in a palace as fine as any,
out there on a great rock in the lake.
Speak to her courteously, and she may give you the sword."
When the lady drew near, Arthur greeted her,
and said he wished the sword might be his, for he had none.
She told him the sword was hers, but bade him go
into the boat moored at the lake's edge and take it.
Merlin and Arthur rowed out in the boat, Arthur took hold of the sword,
and at once the arm disappeared under the water.

When they turned again to the shore, there was no sign of Niniane.
So it was that Arthur received his sword Excalibur.
"Good as the sword is, the scabbard is worth ten of it," said Merlin.
"For as long as you wear it, you will lose no blood,
however badly you are wounded. So keep it with you always."

NOT LONG AFTER THIS ARTHUR MARRIED GWYNEVERE.
Merlin knew of the grief that would come of this in the end,
but he saw that Arthur loved Gwynevere too much
to give her up for any reason,
and so he had to content himself with warning the King.
Gwynevere's father gave Arthur the Round Table as a wedding gift,
and Merlin helped the King to choose his best knights to sit at it.
Among these was Pellinore, who came to court escorting Niniane,
having rescued her from a lawless knight,
who was carrying her off against her will.

Niniane was already wise and skilled in many arts,
but she wished to learn more from Merlin.
At first he diverted her with pretty illusions, conjuring music
from the air and creating garden bowers in the forest.
When he saw that she had a real desire for knowledge, however,
he loved her. He began to teach her all he knew,
and she loved him in return.
They wandered the world together, spending ever less time at court.
Merlin warned Arthur that a time was coming
when he would not be able to return,
but the King could not believe that he could foretell this
yet be unable to prevent it.

THEN NINIANE, IN HER POSSESSIVE LOVE,
asked Merlin to teach her how to bind a man
so that only she could free him.
Although he knew how she meant to use it, Merlin taught her the spell.
They strayed far into the Forest of Broceliande,
and when they were tired, they sat down under a hawthorn tree.
Niniane took Merlin's head in her lap and stroked his hair
until he slept.
Then she wound her veil round the tree,
and stepped round it nine times,
whispering nine times the words Merlin had taught her.
After this she sat down and took his head on her lap again.
When Merlin woke, he seemed to be lying
on a bed in a high tower.
"If you do not stay with me now, you have betrayed me," he said.
"For only you can release me."
"I will not betray you," she said.
Nor did she, but after a time she regretted what she had done,
and would have released him, only the spell was too strong,
and it was beyond her power to undo it.

FOR A LONG TIME ARTHUR'S COURT HEARD NOTHING OF MERLIN.
Then one day when Gawain was riding through the forest,
he heard a voice, like wind rustling the leaves, calling his name.
He was afraid, but then he recognized Merlin's voice
and begged him to show himself.
"You will never see me again," said Merlin.
"And you are the last to hear me.
No one will ever again come to this place, and I can never leave it."
"How can this imprisonment have come upon you,
the wisest of men?" cried Gawain.
"I am also the greatest fool," Merlin replied.
"For I love another more than myself.
I taught my beloved how to bind me to her,
and now I can never be free."

GAWAIN RETURNED TO COURT HEAVY-HEARTED,
and there was great sadness when the King
and his companions
heard that they would never see Merlin again.
It is said that he still sleeps, watched by Niniane,
in his invisible tower,
but that when Arthur wakes,
he too will return to help his country in its greatest need.